This Book is Dedicated to:

Wendy

Kimmy

Cutie

Table of Contents

About the Author.

                                                    Pages 9-11

Acknowledgements.

                                                  Pages 12-13

I Want To Hear From You.

                                                  Page 14-15

Introduction.

                                                  Pages 16-17

My Gift to You!

                                                  Page 18-20

Chapter 1: **It's Only Business!**

                                                  Pages 21-26

Chapter 2: **Constant Cash Flow**

                                                  Pages 27-34

Table of Contents (Continued)

Chapter 3: **Investments**

                        Pages 35-41

Chapter 4: **Hunting for Inventory**

                        Pages 42-48

Chapter 5: **The Negotiator**

                        Pages 49-54

Chapter 6: **The B.R.E.A.D**

                        Pages 55-60

Chapter 7: **W.I.I.F.B & W.I.I.F.S**

                        Pages 61-67

Chapter 8: **The Law of Supply & Demand**

                        Pages 68-73

Chapter 9: **Local Hunting Deals**

                        Pages 74-78

Chapter 10: **Safety First**

                        Pages 79-81

Table of Contents (Continued)

Chapter 11: **_Investment Market, Side By Side Comparison_**

Pages 82-83

Chapter 12: **My Weekly Schedule**

Pages 84-86

Chapter 13: **Whenever However Schedule**

Pages 87-88

Conclusion.

Pages 89-91

Table of Contents (Continued)

Case Study: **Example 1**

                                          Pages 92-96

Case Study: **Example 2**

                                          Pages 97-99

Case Study: **Example 3**

                                          Pages 100-102

Case Study: **Example 4**

                                          Pages 103-105

Case Study: **Example 5**

                                          Pages 106-107

Case Study: **Example 6**

                                          Pages 108-112

Table of Contents (Continued)

Case Study: Example 7

                                          Pages 113-116

Case Study: Example 8

                                          Pages 117-119

Glossary & Acronyms

                                          Page 120

About The Author

M.B. Kim was born in Seoul, South Korea. He was adopted by a wonderful family when he was five years old. This wonderful family raised him to become a great person, and he is very appreciative of this wonderful up-raising because they shared their American lifestyle with him.

At the age of 23, he got married. After five years of being married he had a beautiful child and named her Kimmy. A few years after having her in their lives, M.B. and his wife started having their differences. They started doing their own things and **M. B's lifestyle was increasing so he needed money so, he came up with an idea to stop money from becoming tight.** Therefore, he had to figure out ways to take care of his extra time **and increasing lifestyle since** he wasn't spending it with his wife and daughter.

About The Author (Continued)

Out of necessity, he began to *buy, sell and trade items online for extra cash.* After doing a couple of transactions on a popular website as a hobby, he learned that he could turn this hobby into an extra stream of income, all while *avoiding* working a second part time job for corporate America.

M.B. wants to share with you his experiences, his secrets, and his techniques, to making cash by buying and selling items online in his spare time. From his early days of working as a banker, mortgage industry specialist, and as a consumer, he has always had an interest in becoming an advocate in helping others with improving their lifestyles. This book will teach you how to improve your lifestyle and you will have a blast doing it!

About The Author (Continued)

****In this book, you will learn the successful strategy that he uses to make a constant cash flow of money and how to have fun doing it!* ***

M.B. learned that you either sink or learn to swim- and of course he learned to survive. His life seemed like it has been easy to others, but really, he has had a challenging time in almost everything he's done, but one thing he has learned from his survival is that "**Happiness comes from helping others**".

It is now his time to share with others, his skills and talents that he learned, doing this hobby and part-time job for the last 15 years. Having a constant cash flow is wonderful!!

*****DO YOU WANT IT FOR YOURSELF?** **

Acknowledgements

Thanks to all the years of support, dedication, and encouragement from my daughter **Kimmy, family, friends, and co-workers.** Kimmy and all these people mean the world to me and deserve a special acknowledgement. Thank you, Kimmy, family, friends, and co-workers, for encouraging this long-awaited book on learning the profitable way to buy and resell

Thanks to hundreds of my clients who provided WIIFB and WIIFS (see chapter 7) from all my **past, present, and future deals.** This book was created from the hard work and knowledge that I gained from these transactions. I have learned to adapt in dealing with clients and I learned so much from you all. All of it was and is much appreciated!

Thanks to all of you out there who have made this business what it is today. It is very important that we keep this business going so it can be rewarding and successful for everyone out there.

Acknowledgements (Continued)

And finally, thanks to the millions of you out there who participate in this business- I hope you can take this book and enjoy it. Make it a daily routine for making cash! I am lucky to be able to teach you the tips and tricks of the trade so that you may be successful at this! It really is easy and fun!

I Want to Hear from You!

This is an easy business to learn and once you learn it you will profit from it, and have fun doing it. The success of this business is important on word of mouth, so I would love to hear about your good and bad experiences while buying selling items online. Please don't keep your experience bottled up. Get out there and share it with others- I would love hear from you.

I want you to have constant cash flow to reduce some of your stress. It may help remove some daily obstacles and help you have peace in your life. I know with this book, you can't live a rich life, but you can live a middle-class life comfortably, with an extra, cash-based income.

I Want to Hear from You! (Continued)

Not with just your paycheck from Corporate-America, but your extra-tax-free-cash-on-the-side, or what I like to call my *"Show Me The Flippin' Money"* **Income.**

Email:

showmetheflippinmoney@gmail.com

Introduction

Buying and Reselling items has become a huge industry- one that is now one of the biggest arenas for extra income in the marketplace. Whether you are a beginner or have experience, you will learn from one of the best on how to make (and keep) constant cash to support your lifestyle.

This book was created out of my personal business, and the excitement in the market of buying and reselling. I have been doing this for quite a while and I want all of you to constantly refer to this book as a **how-to guide**, every step of the way. Study it so that you can implement all the suggestions and ideas immediately and start making some great money!

Introduction (Continued)

Sure, there are many successful books out there on this topic, but I believe *this* book has the edge on the market because I share the particular skills, techniques, and secrets that will make you a SUCCESS! When you begin this business, others will admire you and look to you for their own success. Don't be shy-introduce them to my book.

By reading, examining, and studying this book, you will be able to implement a strategy immediately and start turning your *weak* cash flow into *successful* cash flow. At the same time, you'll be having fun doing it. Remember the acronyms "WIIFB" and "WIIFS" (see Chapter 7) as a seller/buyer to determine on how much you make on a product. The more you make, the more "Wow" it becomes!!

My Gift 2 "U"

15 years ago, I needed extra money. I had extra time on my hands and was barely keeping my head above water **with my social life.** So, I started a fun hobby. I began to buy and then resell popular items online. After a couple of successful deals, I figured out that this could become a fun and exciting way to make extra income. This is so easy! So, I said to myself, "This is a great alternative to working a part-time job". Making money this way, I can choose my own schedule- I have no boss to report to, and best of all, I determine how much I want to make. Work smarter, not harder!

The past 15 years I have learned a lot in this process. I have learned what is hot and what is not hot on the market. I met a lot of people, and I got to use my smart phone and **technology gadget's at full capacity.**

My Gift 2 "U" (Continued)

But best of all, I've learned what it is like to have a constant cash flow, to have extra money around, and how to live my "Awesome social life". All of us need extra cash or extra income; we can use these funds to spoil ourselves or for peace of mind. We can afford new hobbies, share with others, and possibly pay off our debt quicker, or to pay for some extra bills, or even have emergency money. It's been great to know that with this extra avenue of income I personally have not ever worried about having cash! If you take all the skills that I've learned in the past 15 years and implement them, I guarantee you'll have fun at this, and you will be able to reap the rewards- once you put my book to work, of course.

I want you to know that I've lived my whole life helping myself, family, and others close to me, and now it is time to for me to share my success.

My Gift 2 "U" (Continued)

Remember, if you want to make this constant income and be able to help yourself, your family and others, you will need to implement this book immediately as a part-timer, flipping items online.

I've been able to share my concepts of constant cash flow with important people around me, and it has been great sharing my money! It has allowed me to live a step up above the middle class. This is my gift to you, the gift is security and happiness!

"Please enjoy my gift to you! Put it to work immediately!

Chapter 1: **It's Only Business**

So, what is our business? How do we make money? Here's the deal- you will simply buy items online and resell them to others. We call it *Flippin*. IT'S THAT SIMPLE! How is this possible? That is simple, too. The market of buyers and sellers is crowded with people who are willing to sell items for less than what they are *really* worth. There are also many buyers who are willing to buy items for what they *are* worth! The difference in these values is what we are aiming for-it is PROFIT! We help people sell their items, and we help people find items that they want.

So how is this possible, you ask? The reason could be obvious or difficult to define. There are thousands of reasons why people buy and sell used items. Sellers and buyers have different motivations. Sellers may be looking to clear out extra space in their home, apartment, garage, office, etc.

Chapter 1: **It's Only Business (Continued)**

They may be "hard up" for cash, or they may just simply be tired of the item, or can't use it. Think of a kid who got a guitar for Christmas, but quickly realized it was too difficult to learn, or he might be more interested in playing the drums. This person has no use for the item, and doesn't particularly care about how much he sells it for. This is where YOU come in! But, you must think like a business person. This is very important to remember when you are dealing with these types of business transactions. **You may look at these transactions as personal but remember always these are only business transactions. This is why you will immediately need** to learn a business mindset. "Remember these transactions are business only." So remember to buy low and to sell high (more on this later).

Chapter 1: **It's Only Business (Continued)**

If you keep this business mindset strong, you should be able to take these skills and keep a constant part-time income and have fun doing it. Remember if you're not having fun doing this, then this is probably not something that you should be doing, so I highly recommend that you start a little at a time and as you start building your portfolio, then you can increase your portfolio as your business mindset improves.

These are only business transactions so don't lose sleep over it or stress out over it- complete the transaction and then move on to the next transaction. To help out with your business mindset, remember that many **corporations in the world can make up to 200% to 300% profit on products they have sold.**

Chapter 1: *It's Only Business (Continued)*

So while engaging in this business, you should not feel guilty at all. Remember as a strong flipper, you determine how much you save when you buy and how much you will profit when you sell. The stronger the business mindset, the more profitable it becomes.

Once you become successful in this business then you should share this with others. By sharing this with others you will help them and also you may learn from them.

I have learned so much from others involved in this business and also from family, friends, and co-workers. At first I thought I could do this business by myself and I did but as time went on I learned that others could help me on the way. From all of the help I have provided to them and from the help they have provided to me I was able to learn not to take these transactions personal and to learn the business mind set.

Chapter 1: *It's Only Business (Continued)*

At first I was sad making a lot of money off of others but in Learning from Corporate America and seeing others do this I have gained happiness from doing these business transactions.

The strongest thing I learned was that I was helping others and others were helping me and this is what business is all about and keeps our eco system living. I'm a very kind person because the money I was making from my business was helping others. I was able to make contributions to society by buying, helping, and mentoring others. My happiness from this has made me a better person today. Without having this business mind set I would've sunk a long time of go and given up on this and therefore this book would have never been published.

It's sad to say that Corporate America could've made lots of money off of me by having me work for them part time but I chose this fun Hobby/Part-time Job.

Chapter 1: <u>It's Only Business (Continued)</u>

I know my skills would've made part time Corporate America lots of profits and I'm so glad that I didn't work for Corporate America part-time 15 years ago. Enough about me and how I learned to become a business mindset. It is human to have a conscious on some deals that you buy low and make lots of money selling high. Don't be sad when you do this because think about all of the things you can now do with your profits. I recommend you do what good Corporate America does with there income. They put it back into the business or share it wisely with others. A understanding of the business mindset will help you become successful from this book in your deals and best of all it will help you with why you bought this book it's a

"<u>Constant Cash Flow.</u>"

Chapter 2: **Constant Cash Flow**

We all want to make extra money and we all want it to be a constant flow, so here's how to make the money flow constant.

Once you start buying items cheap and then flipping them for a higher value, your cash flow will increase. You can turn around and buy another similar priced item **with the profits, or keep the profits,** or you could buy something a little bit more expensive and flip that for even more money! I would save a little for fun or for a rainy day or Reinvest it back into your part-time business, or you can just keep some of the money for monthly cash flow and the rest you can reinvest into more inventory and success.

When you reinvest it's like playing with the house's money, so to speak and everybody likes to play with house money.

So let's get started! Here's how you can start a constant cash-based business.

Chapter 2: **<u>Constant Cash Flow (Continued)</u>**

To make this a successful program, you will need to **sign up for buying/reselling websites and for many buying/reselling** apps as you can manage. The more you can learn to manage, the more transactions you can engage in, the more inventory and sales that you will be able to build up.

This leads to a constant cash flow. Ideally you would want to have many items available to sell at any one time. Think of a convenience store- they tend to sell hundreds of different items, all at a mark-up. But they do not depend on selling *just* candy, or *just* gasoline.

You can either start your business small or you can start big. You determine on how fast you want to grow your business, and you determine how much money you want to make.

Chapter 2: <u>Constant Cash Flow (Continued)</u>

If you have the immediate cash flow then you can make large transactions and potentially turn it into one big profit. But I recommend you buy lots of small items that you can flip quickly and make a constant cash flow. Personally, I have never bought big item transactions. I've always bought small items that I know that I can flip to make double or triple their value. Remember- be wise in your decisions, because it's possible that your inventory will not be moving or you'll be sitting on lost cash for a while, so be cautious in your business dealings! But, if you play your cards right you'll be able to flip an item and make a profit to spend freely on more inventory, yourself, family or whatever is important to you.

If you do sit on items that aren't moving, then you will start to lower the price a little at a time and even sometimes you will sell the item for what you bought it for.

Chapter 2: **Constant Cash Flow (Continued)**

If the item isn't selling, then maybe you need to remove it and re add it and use a different market strategy. Like new pictures or new marketing words. I have sat on products for a few months and doing this change they have then sold. You can always make your money back on other items your selling.

For a constant cash flow you will need to constantly watch your inventory. Doing the "BREAD" (Chapter 9) and other creative measures will make money for you. There will be slow times in this business and you should plan for them to help your constant cash flow. In Chapter 5 this will show you how to prepare for these slow times and to maximize your dollars during the busy time.

Chapter 2: **<u>Constant Cash Flow (Continued)</u>**

If you can learn to use these skills at an optimized level, then you will not have to worry about the cash. Your items will sale if your just do what I have shared in this book. I know this because I have taken all of my business to another level.

In keeping a constant cash flow you will need to learn to play with house money and also put some of your money away for rainy days. If you see that your house money is getting low from buying too much and not from selling, then you will need to focus on your inventory and stop buying for now. Who wants to sit on items and possibly slow down their cash flow.

In having this cash flow successful you will need to work this out with your significant other if there is one. Because, they may want to help you and also it is there cash in some situations. In talking to them about this cash flow you should share this book with them and then they will understand the business you are in and how it can help out your money situations.

Chapter 2: **Constant Cash Flow (Continued)**

This book is for families to get a constant cash flow and a piece of mind on their financial income without having to work outside of the home in Corporate America Part-Time. Part-Time jobs are good for a constant cash flow but remember you have to work really hard to make any money after paying taxes and their schedules. This constant cash flow is on your own time and it can be done from anywhere you are.

I want families to spend more time with each other and not have to worry about bosses and other co-workers. All of us already work hard enough at our full time jobs. Plus, with this constant cash flow job you will not need to worry about it at tax time. You could even open a safe investment account and help your constant cash flow gain even more money.

Chapter 2: **Constant Cash Flow (Continued)**

Putting your money to work for you is like a double constant cash flow. The rich get richer because they have a constant cash flow from their business and also make money from their constant cash flow.

Let's learn how your business mindset and constant cash flow compare to the current investment markets.

Chapter 3: **Investment**

Every item that you buy is an investment. The hope is to get some profit, even if it a small one. The potential to make easy money is huge. But a word of caution- every investment has its risks. There are all kinds of risks in this line of work. You will learn how to get around these risks. Let's talk about a few of them.

The risk of spoilage. This is the risk that your item will cease to exist in sellable form. This is one reason why we do not deal in food items. If we were in the business of selling food, like a grocery store, we would have to mark down our items for quick sale. Therefore, bananas and cilantro are dirt cheap. Therefore, you should never try to flip something that will spoil.

Chapter 3: **Investment (Contiued)**

Breakage is another risk to our business. Think of precious breakable items like pottery, items with many moving parts, picture frames, etc. You break it, you bought it, and now it's worthless! In this fashion, we can see that the risk in the flip is 100% of your purchase price. You lose it all if it breaks, and you cannot sell broken items. If you don't believe me, check out used cars for sale on craigslist under $1,000! The items that you choose to flip must be seen as investments. You must see the potential reward *and* the risk involved. Which brings me to my next point. This one is great advice for life. BUY LOW, SELL HIGH. It sounds obvious but you would be amazed at how many flippers buy items at normal-to-high prices and realize that they cannot mark things up for any profit. As the old saying goes, you make the money on the buy, not the sale.

Chapter 3: **Investment (Continued)**

Now that we have gotten the risks out of the way, we can focus on the purpose of this book. The reward!

Let's say you are searching your favorite sites and you see the same model of television at different prices on each site. Say it's $100 dollars in one marketplace, and $75 dollars on the other. Which TV would you buy? The $75 TV, of course! This is a wonderful way to learn about the market for the item you will sell. Given that the TV is worth $100, you rush out to get the cheaper TV, and immediately place your ad at the higher price of $100.

But, wait, you ask! Why doesn't the seller just sell the TV at the higher price?

Chapter 3: *Investment (Continued)*

How often does this happen? Believe me my friends, it happens every day in every city. The seller may be very motivated for the cash in hand. If you are hungry, you cannot eat a television! People have water and electricity bills to pay. They have car notes and insurance and child care to pay for. These things are more important than television! These are the same people who are buying electronics that they cannot afford the minute their tax refunds are in hand!

In the example above, you would buy the $75 TV and sell it for $100-the same price as the other TV. Maybe you sell it first because you write a better ad. Maybe you sell it first because your ad is newer than the other guys (see the B.R.E.A.D. Chapter).

Chapter 3: **_Investment (Continued)_**

Remember- this other seller is your competition, so fight for your profit! You can also undercut him by $5, and take $95. Or you could offer the buyer a free remote or some other accessory like plasma screen cleaning wipes. You could also deliver the item to him and hold strong at $100.

Now, I know what you're thinking, it sounds easy, but it's only $25 dollars in profit. Listen to me now. You can do that flip in an hour or less. And you can repeat it as often as you like. How many part time jobs do you know of that will pay you $25 and let you work for 1 hour and quit? And think about this- $25 in profit on a $75 investment? That is a 33% return in less than a day. Never in a million years will you make that kind of *annual* return in your 401k, your grandma's coin collection, or a house flip!

Chapter 3: **Investment (Continued)**

Learn the market that you are in. Spend some time looking at the marketplace. Notice what sells and what doesn't. Notice how quickly underpriced items get bought up, and notice when someone is asking too much for their item- they will repost it at a lower price, or it will go unsold for months. Once you learn what a good deal is, you will be able to jump on it, and PROFIT! Think like an investor, think about your risk, and think about what an item could be sold for.

Here are some examples to help you get an idea of how much money you can make.

Item	Buy Price	Sell Price	% Return	$ Profit	Time
Guitar	$149	$375	152%	$226	4 Days
Stereo	$25	$60	140%	$35	1 Day
Leather Jacket	$10	$40	300%	$30	6 Hours
Beanie Baby	$40	$200	450%	$180	1 Hour
TV	$75	$100	33%	$25	1 Day
Weed Whacker	$20	$45	125%	$25	4 Days
Laptop	$340	$600	76%	$260	1 Day
Bicycle	$20	$65	225%	$45	2 Days
Totals	$679	$1,505	122%	$826	4-10 Days

Chapter 4: **Hunting for Inventory**

Let the fun begin and let's go hunting for inventory! As explained in the prior chapters you want to sign up or download as many resell apps as you can on your mobile devices. Remember it's not about how hard you work these days but it's all about working smarter for big returns. Start with **Craigslist, LetGo, Ebay, OfferUp, 5Mile, Facebook Garage Sale Sites,** etc. The more marketplaces that you have available, the more information that is available to you. Also, you will be able to gain access to more pricing information, and have more choices on what to buy and sell. You can also buy items on one site, and sell them on others.

Determine how much you can spend and start out small. Start with one or two items, and as your money returns to you in the form of profits, you can begin to increase the number of items you can flip at one time.

Chapter 4: **Hunting for Inventory (Continued)**

From the sales, you may want to invest in more inventory; smaller items have the potential to make more than double and triple your returns but remember, the more you sell the small items for the more money you can put towards purchasing bigger items. Once again, our big items pose a higher risk but have more potential to make a larger one-time payout, which could be well worth it.

Every time you are working this part time job you will need to make hunting for inventory a personal goal. For example, you will want to make offers on about 40-50 items. I believe that the more items you make low offers on, the chances of getting a bite will increase. Remember, you only need a few people to bite on those low offers.

Chapter 4: **_Hunting for Inventory (Continued)_**

Throw as much mud on the wall as you can, because personally you will never know what will stick! Just go out and have fun doing this part time job! Let's go hunting and make those offers.

By the way, some items you may just want to keep yourself or for your family and friends. It's all up to you if you want to sell it for business or to keep it for yourself.

While hunting for items to flip, you might find an item that you can possibly add an accessory to, in order to increase its value. For example, in an iPhone sale, you could add a cheap charger, a cheap case or a cheap accessory to the deal to help sell your inventory. This is called *facilitating the sale*. Think of this as an incentive to help your buyer buy your product and not the other guy's.

Chapter 4: **Hunting for Inventory (Continued)**

So, when you're looking at these ads remember if you see that the phone does not have a charger or a case, maybe you could add these and keep your price high. Complete package deals sell so quickly in this business! So, if you can buy something that needs accessories, you can cheaply add something to it to complete it. You will benefit and possibly sell that for a higher price. Guitar for sale? Throw in some new strings. Selling a bicycle, add an air pump or tire repair kit. These items add convenience and value. They also help you stay strong on your price when the buyer begins to negotiate.

Hunting for your inventory should be done in a fun, creative, and safe way. This is one of the most exciting things you will do to start your inventory. In the hunt you will need to be a strong.

Chapter 4: **Hunting for Inventory (Continued)**

The stronger you are the more flexible you will have in the item you are selling. The stronger you are the more profit and bigger wow it will become.

Don't just limit your self to just the internet in finding inventory. You can find items in your own environment and also fro other paths like explained (Chapter 7). Go into this with an open mind and this is where you might spend most of your time in this business. The more time you spend smartly in this the less you will have to work harder. Remember it's all about working smarter and not harder. I've been in corporate America and I have learned a lot especially its not the hard workers that succeed because, its all about the smart workers. People think it's the hard workers succeeding but it is really the smarter workers succeeding.

Chapter 4: *Hunting for Inventory (Continued)*

In locating your inventory and if you get board just then take a small break and let your mind and eyes do some recovering. You will be surprised on what a fresh set of eyes and energy can do for you in your searching. You can even take this business on the go. By, taking it to a coffee shop, work, family event, or even on the deck of your home.

When hunting your success is determined on how and when you find time to do this business. For example: I look for items to buy in the morning and then set appointments for buying and selling the afternoon when I get off of work or I do vice versa.
This part-time job is made not to be stressful but to be fun and an anytime schedule. I really look for business 24/7 hours a day but only when I have time. I really don't consider finding items to buy as job but as a fun hobby.

Chapter 4: **_Hunting for Inventory (Continued)_**

I try to look how it will help me and others in their daily lives and events. When working on your inventory you will need to find items that will help others and also are in demand. So I would recommend watching social media, your family, and friends. These avenues of observance will help you in locating inventory that will sell quickly and not occupy space.

The success of this business is not to become a hoarder but to learn to buy items that will move in and out of your business. This is why I recommend items that do not take up much space. Once it starts to take up space you will then have to liquidate for lower prices. I want you
to know that you won't have to worry about that if you put this book to your full business concept. Now that you are a successful hunter t is now time to move on to how to become a successful Negotiator.

Chapter 5: **The Negotiator**

Here's how to negotiate for small dollar items. Look for all potential items on your resell apps or websites that you signed up for. Everyone likes it when you deal with numbers, so here is an example: Let's say you find $100 item for sale- *you* start the negotiations at $30. Remember, don't go higher than $60 in your final negotiations. The seller is already selling the item cheaper than retail price. His $100 item possibly retails for $150 plus tax. Plus, he or she knows that *the asking price is never the final price*. Do not ever accept the seller's asking price.

The stronger you are in the negotiating process, the more potential for higher profit. You can always walk away from the deal and wait for someone who will pay your asking price. Let them know that! Don't forget that you can never sell something above the retail price unless it is a highly collectible item, so it is crucial that you negotiate your deals. The profit is made when you buy items cheaply!

Chapter 5: **The Negotiator (Continued)**

Here's one trick that I learned in the negotiation process. I call it "The Upper Hand". Have your friend call you while buyer is haggling with you. He can pretend like he is an interested buyer and willing to pay full price, no questions asked. Let the haggler hear you on the phone. This trick worked out for me once when I sold a Honda Civic. My phone was exploding with calls from very interested parties; these were buyers lined up to take the deal. Once the buyer saw that he had no negotiating power, he offered me $200 dollars more than my asking price, and I was on to the next deal. By the way, if you have placed an ad on an item, and you get more than say 40 calls on the item, *your price is too low*. Consider raising the price, you won't be sorry!

Chapter 5: **_The Negotiator (Continued)_**

So why will the seller sell to you for a low price? How can you get the best deals, knowing that a profit is around the corner? You will need to read the details of the seller's advertisement; this will give you negotiating power. The details will describe how motivated the sellers are.

Chapter 5: *The Negotiator (Continued)*

Here is a list of what to look for when the sellers want to get rid of the product fast and cheap-

- "Need money immediately."
- "Must get rid of today."
- "I don't want it or need it anymore."
- "We are moving."
- "It is a sentimental item that I just want to get rid of."
- "I have two of these."
- "It was a gift; I really don't want or need it"
- "It's taking up space"

Chapter 5: **_The Negotiator (Continued)_**

Here is a list of keywords to search for incredible deals!

- Divorce
- Baby
- Apartment
- New house
- Bills
- New job
- Relocating

Here's another important tip that you need to know. The seller may want to get rid of the item because they have had the ad up for a long time, so you'll need to look how long the ad has been posted. For example, if the ad has been posted for a long time they want to negotiate and possibly get rid of that product. At this point they just want the item gone. Lucky You!

Chapter 5: **_The Negotiator (Continued)_**

Just go out there and offer ridiculous prices on these resell apps or websites that you signed up for. If you use any of these negotiations tactics in this chapter, you will be able to build your inventory quickly, and for real cheap.

Chapter 6: **B.R.E.A.D.**

B.R.E.A.D. stands for BOOST, REBOOT, EDIT, ADD, DELETE. This is our acronym for the process that we take to make sure our advertisement is seen by the most eyes possible. Every day, hundreds of novice sellers just post an ad to sell an item, and then they never maintain the ad. They never come back to it. They wonder why the item never sells.

Do you know the average amount of time someone spends searching for something that they need? It's not long, maybe a few minutes. This means that the first few listings will be gaining the most attention. You need to **BOOST** your ad to the top of the list! Especially when you are selling a unique item; sometimes people don't search using keywords, they will just jump in and start scrolling through.

A **REBOOST** is when you publish the listing again. Maybe you will change a few minor things, or maybe you will try another marketplace.

Chapter 6: **B.R.E.A.D.(Continued)**

EDIT, is obvious. You change the general look of the ad to get more attention. Maybe your first approach wasn't the best, so you try again. Also, you can add in more pictures or details of the item. Also think about dropping that $100 item to $99. This is a great trick to sell it quicker!

ADD additional information to your listing. Also add it to other marketplaces. Some items just sell better on different apps! Jewelry might not sell well on craigslist, but may sell for top dollar on Ebay!

DELETE means to remove your ad completely. You may need to do this if the application does not allow you to keep boosting and editing your listings. Delete the ad and start again. In general, you will get more attention if you add B.R.E.A.D. to your business. Then you will have some dough in your pocket!

Marketing a product is very important. How do you display your inventory? Let's say you just bought an item for $50 but the seller had it out there for $100. If it was new it would retail for $150 plus tax. So, you're asking price should start at $125 to $150.

Chapter 6: **B.R.E.A.D. (Continued)**

On your listing, you may want to post the retail price plus tax, because the potential buyers can see the retail price as compared to your asking price so the buyer will *know* that they're getting a deal. If the item has a model number, include that in your description so that they can compare a retail advertisement to the one you're selling. This is a very useful tactic, especially if you were not able to get the product cheaply.

Words are very powerful. When you are creating your ad, you will need to put in some important marketing verbiage to help sell your inventory. Avoid using the descriptive words that you searched earlier when buying the product; that might show your new buyers that you are a motivated seller. You are not eager to sell cheaply or quickly. You are out to make PROFIT. Create a sense that the buyer needs you more than you need them.

Chapter 6: **B.R.E.A.D. (Continued)**

Focus on the value of the item and how the buyer will use it. Mention details that make the product unique or special. Your ad is what creates value in the eyes of buyers. The more skillfully-worded your ad is, the more profit you will receive. And another thing- spellcheck your listing! When I see someone who doesn't know the difference between the words "sell" and "sale", I know I'm dealing with someone who can be haggled. Do not project this image! Avoid misspelled words and always use complete sentences. Utilize pictures, technical information, and anything else that creates value in the eyes of the buyer. Now that you've posted the item with that successful marketing verbiage, you'll need to know this important marketing strategy.

Chapter 6: **B.R.E.A.D. (Continued)**

You will need to ADD, BOOST, and EDIT your items a couple times a day because it moves it up in the chain of priority for potential clients to always see your inventory ad. Important if you don't consistently Add, Boost and Edit your ad, then potential buyers will not see your items. Then this will hurt your opportunity for being a successful seller.

When you Add, Boost and Edit your inventory, don't do all of your inventory at the same time. If you do this, your inventory will clump up of all your items on the website or on the app, and potential buyers will skip over your cluster of ads. Go in there and just do a few at a time. Stop posting for a few minutes, then go back in and do more. You cannot make it seem like you are a steady business. Just try to blend in with the other average sellers.

Chapter 6: **B.R.E.A.D. (Continued)**

Like I have said in prior chapters this is another very important aspect of your business. You must once again do the BREAD process all of the time. I can't tell you have often after I have done the BREAD I start to get inundated with interests of my items. I have also received many of my successful sales from the BREAD.

After being successful with the BREAD make sure you get up and have a drink umm like a break. This will help your BREAD digest. Don't eat all of your bread at once as explained

prior in this chapter. Remember do a little at a time and by dong this you won't look like a seller and just like a regular person these websites and apps.

Chapter 7: **WIIFB & WIIFS**

W.I.I.F.B stands for "What's in it for buyer" & W.I.I.F.S stands for "What's in it for seller". Your sole purpose as a buyer and reseller is to find situations where both the buyer and seller feel like they both got a great deal. The deal doesn't always have to be in monetary terms for others, but it does have to be for you. Sellers often just want to get rid of these items. They are making room in their house, garage, office, or business. That's a deal for them.

These acronyms were learned from a friend of mine. He would always use the acronym WIFFM. This stands for "What's in it for me". I would always use this in my daily interactions with friends and family. So, I decided to implement these fun acronyms into my business.

Chapter 7: **WIIFB & WIIFS (Continued)**

Always think these acronyms' through when buying and selling for our business. When hunting and negotiating I always think "WIIFB" because the stronger this thinking the better it looks for you as "WIIFS".

Remembering the WIIFB and WIIFS acronyms will help you buy and sell *faster*. This will help you save time, effort and money. The secret is to find Win-Win situations for everyone. As a Buyer and a Seller, stay strong in your negotiating power. Remember, the stronger you are, the more profit you have a potential to make.

The stronger you become as a "WIIFB" the more cushion you will have on the back end of the transaction. So if you are weak you are not going to have much breathing room as "WIIFS.

Chapter 7: **WIIFB & WIIFS (Continued)**

This has been learned from many prior transactions and the quicker you learn this concept the more you will save as a "WIIFB" and the more and less stressful it will be as "WIIFS". By the way you can have real fun as a "WIIFB by getting items cheap and then you will even have as a "WIIFFS" wow moment.

As a WIIFB you do not have to buy the item immediately. If the Seller won't back down them move on to another item. You may want to check back with the WIIFB a couple of times and see if they have had a change in there negotiating. If you make a compulsive by and don't work this strategy, we have taught you this could be a sign of weakness and could become a trend for you.

Chapter 7: **WIIFB &WIIFS (Continued)**

So it is better not to give in too early as a WIIFB. As WIIFB's and WIIFS you must learn early to set good habits just like in life. The better your habits the easier your part-time job will be and also the more fun it will b for you. It takes just a few times to gain a bad habit and people don't think of it as a problem but it can and will be a big problem as you run your business/hobby to make a constant cash flow. If you know that transactions as WIIFB's and WIIFS are going the right way you planned it quickly learning to buy or sell quickly and then move on just like we taught you in chapter 1 – "It's Business Only."

As WIIFS's and WIIFB's I learned to be patient, passive, and even play a dumb card once in a while. It's all about working smarter and not harder. Hard working WIIFB's and WIIFS's do well in this business but it is the smarter ones that are beating the hard working one's. The hard working ones in this business work about double the time and put in the double stress and pains.

Chapter 7: **WIIFB & WIIFS (Continued)**

I would like to say that I use to be a hard worker only and I figured out late in life that it wasn't really going anywhere so now I'm smarter at what I do. I don't want you to think that Harder workers are looked down upon but they are kind of. The smarter workers are somewhat liked and disliked but that is life. I want you as WIIFB and WIIFS to put to work both of these skills. Work hard and smart and you will be successful in this field. I also wanted you to learn to use networking in this business. You can team up with other WIIFB and WIIFS. Have other WIIFB and WIIFS buy and sell some of your products and share the profits with each other. I have done this many times because this broadens you buying and selling areas and this will help out on time and money. With this business strategy you may make less in transactions but you may sell more and remember all of the small transactions can all add up to your benefit.

Chapter 7: **WIIFB & WIIFS (Continued)**

I have teamed up with co-workers in the past and we have made this a fun little business at work and on our personal time. Remember: The more creative you are with this business the less hard you have to work and in a sense you are working smarter.

Time is Money and money is time as WIIFB and WIIFS's. The reason you got into this business was to learn to maximize your buying and selling powers. So learn to use social networking with anyone you can but be careful not to ruin your social network if it is really close to you. Money is not worth losing your social network. I've always given just a little more to the social network to help me out in the long run. In this process I have grown and learned from them and others. All I can say is learning from other WIIFB and WIIFS's is a wonderful and need experience in your business.

Chapter 7: **WIIFB & WIIFS (Continued)**

Here is an important skill to remember. Let's use a strong seller, for example. Your product retails for $150 plus tax and you're selling it for $125, (you bought it for $50) and another buyer offers you $100. You can take the $100 and say to the him, "I guess I will take the small loss", or you can stay strong at $125 and say to the buyer that you are low already, in fact
lower than what it is retailing for. Maximize your profits by staying strong, but if you really want to get rid of the product, go ahead and sell it. But make sure that you make double your money, or close to it. You may also want to put in your ad that "low ballers will be ignored". This works well. Your ability to create Win-Win situations will help you pay the bills with this book!

Chapter 8: **The Law of Supply & Demand**

Let's capitalize on the law of supply and demand. What is this law? The law of supply and demand states that if there is a high demand, or desire for a product, the higher the price can be. The price rises naturally. Therefore, the lower the demand, the lower the price.

Demand is always searching for balance with the supply, or the number of similar products available. Think of it this way. Let's say that a legitimate medical report is released tomorrow that says that green apples cure cancer. Everyone would buy up all the green apples. Since apples take time to grow, the demand would be higher than the supply available, so people would happily pay a little more for the benefit of the special cure for cancer!

Chapter 8: **The Law of Supply & Demand (Continued)**

In a sense, the price of the apple would be bid up like the price of a custom classic car at a car auction, until the price would roughly be a representation of the value of the cure for cancer. You can see this in home sales, stock prices, memorabilia, collectibles and anything rare or irreplaceable.

Have you ever paid $5 dollars for a bottle of water on a sweltering day at a carnival or concert, knowing that you can go down the street and get the same bottle of water for $1? Sometimes the law of supply and demand is controlled by convenience or by situations. Your job is to identify these situations and profit from them!

So how do we make this work in our flipping business? Seasonal deals are very important for our type of business. We need to sell certain things at the right time of year.

Chapter 8: **The Law of Supply & Demand (Continued)**

For example: Super Bowl, St. Patrick's Day, Mother's Day, Valentine's Day, Father's Day, Fourth of July, Easter, Back-to-school, start of summer, Halloween, Thanksgiving, Christmas, national holiday, Chinese New Year, whatever!

Let's take the Super Bowl for example. The Super Bowl is one of the biggest and most popular time of the year that people want to buy TVs and entertainment gadgets, so you may want to buy some TV and entertainment gadgets for cheap a month before the event, and then two weeks before the event.

You may want to start selling those items for a higher price but lower than what they are retailing for. Demand for good TV's is *high* in this time of year, because it is winter and people spend a lot of time indoors. Therefore, the price stays high!

Chapter 8: **The Law of Supply & Demand (Continued)**

Just before summertime you may want to buy lots of kids toys, outdoor equipment, barbecues or summer clothing so when summer comes people will buy those items from you! Just like a retail store loads up on Christmas decorations, you'll be there to load up on fun summer items, ready for sale! For small holidays, you may want to build up your inventory and then sell it for cheap a couple weeks before that small holiday.

For a major holiday, you may want to buy the items a couple months before and then sell them during that holiday season. Remember, this is the biggest time of the year for buyers and sellers. Just because you're building your inventory up doesn't mean that you can't buy the items for your family members, friends or co-workers and you can give them out as nice gifts. This always makes you a hit!

Chapter 8: **The Law of Supply & Demand (Continued)**

Watch out for seasonal sporting events like football season, soccer season, baseball season, cheerleading season, basketball season. Once again, these are events that you may want to buy inexpensive items for, and then sell them just before the season or during the season (for a higher price, of course). **The Law of Supply and demand also can determine on how much you have to spend and how much you have to make.** The more of the inventory you have the higher the demand of your dinero will be and the less you have the to make dinero. Be careful not to put too much of your money into this law. Cash flow is a maker or breaker of this business. You must have cash flow when the demand is low and high so you can always buy and sell items in your inventory.

Before you buy an item test the market out. Post the add before you even buy the product.

Chapter 8: *The Law of Supply & Demand (Continued)*

I have done this many times and before I even buy the product I have a seller in hand. It's an awesome feeling to have a seller before you even buy the product.

This is where you are ahead of the Law and Supply theory. Sometimes I will even keep the ad out there after I have sold it. In this situation I had a buyer find my old ad and I didn't have the product but I pushed myself and I found the product. I done hundreds of transactions even before I have the product in my hands. This is an awesome and important way of supporting Law and Demand.

Chapter 9: **Local Hunting Deals**

You probably thought that I forgot this, but I didn't! Remember, 'tis the season for garage sales, yard sales, estate sales, events, secondhand stores, goodwill, and etc. Be creative in searching for local hunting deals. You can go and buy stuff inexpensively at these events and then once again turn it around and make a profit off them. This is probably the easiest way to make money. The key here is that you are buying on the cheap, and then expanding your coverage area by posting these items online. People selling in these lines o f business usually want to get rid of the items cheap for many reasons. Find it and make some ridiculous offers. Find unique items that can usually sell at high profits in this manner. Items usually that have never been opened, missing just one little item to complete, need a little TLC, or look easy to fix.

Chapter 9: **Local Hunting Deals (Continued)**

I heard a story one time of an old lady who sold a dusty guitar out of her attic at a garage sale one time, for the price of ten dollars. The buyer eagerly went home and looked up the value of the guitar, which happened to be a rare 1950's Les Paul Goldtop, worth $50,000. You might not sale it for this amount but you catch my drift. I have heard of many success stories like this and this is what keeps the art of Flippin' going.

When you buy from these places, you shouldn't feel bad for buying items cheap. You are helping the businesses or individuals by getting rid of inventory. When they have inventory, they must pay for the storage expenses. Real Estate is not cheap. Not just for real estate purposes but it's nice and convenient to have the freed up space if it is in your yard, home, or other rooms. Insurance on that property is another holding cost and also the possibility of loosing the item, breaking it, or even losing its value.

Chapter 9: **Local Hunting Deals (Continued)**

Perhaps we are always needing the extra space in our lives or we really need to move or get rid of it. You are just helping these businesses or individuals by moving their stuff that they don't need or want any longer.

It is good to know that when you find an item, before you buy it, you should go to the Internet and Google it and find out what you can possibly buy that item for. This will give you an idea of what you could possibly sell that item for. Do a little research before buying the item and you'll know if you can get it for a cheap price and be able to flip that item.

Doing the much needed research prior to buying helps out in the long run. If you buy a couple of items from that person too they might even give you a better deal. Time after time I have bought lots of items and the seller has given me a big discount.

Chapter 9: <u>**Local Hunting Deals (Continued)**</u>

If the seller doesn't like our price, make a strategic move and be creative in having the seller meet your price. Don't just research how low you can get the item for but also look and see what you can get for this item like on the resale sites.

Research on the selling sites what they are selling for and how long the items have been on the market. IF the item you are looking to buy has been long on these resale sites then maybe the price of the item is too high or the person selling it doesn't know how to market it and sell it.

In these lines of business, it is great to know what the market is selling these items for and how they are doing. You don't want to buy inventory that you will be sitting long on. So do your research diligently and by doing this you will be able to profit the most and also not sit on the items too long.

Chapter 9: **Local Hunting Deals (Continued)**

These are also great lines to get cheap items for friends, family, co-workers, and etc. If you see any special occasion coming up, you can get them the best deals here. Remember to only buy items that look new or you can put a little TLC into. I have done this many times and I have looked like I spend a fortune and cared about the person. You will be the talk of the party and it will put a smile on you and who you are buying it for.

Lastly, always think cautiously! Impulse buying can hurt you! Think it through before you pull the trigger!

Chapter 10: *Safety First*

I cannot stress how very important this is, because when dealing with buying stuff and selling stuff some people are shady and some people are good souls. Always think **"Safety First"**! Meet in a safe place that is lit up and possibly during daytime or where there are a lot of people. Make sure you tell someone where you're going and only do local transactions, *cash only*. When in doubt, meet at a designated *Safe Trade Station*. This is a police station, municipal building, or other **public place that no crook would dare to go**. The minute your counterparty agrees to meet you there, it is almost a guaranteed safe transaction.

Note: if you buy something that is malfunctioning, or broken, the police are not going to do anything. Small transactions that are not reputable, however distasteful, are considered petty crimes. Remember, be careful! Test every item.

Chapter 10: **Safety First (Continued)**

If it is electrical, plug it in, turn it on. Use it and make sure every feature on it works. Given that you have asked the buyer about the condition before you make the drive, hold the seller to it. Question them as many times as needed. Read their faces and their demeanor. Your potential risk is 100% of the cost of the item, so make sure you know what you are buying!

If you're buying the cell phone, make sure you meet them at the service provider like **AT&T or Verizon**. If you're buying an Apple product, you may want to meet them at the Apple Store. If you're buying an electronic item, you may want to test the unit at a retail shop before buying it from the potential seller.

Here's a Pro Tip: buy a power convertor for your car! This converts the power from your cigarette lighter receptacle to household electricity. Now you can test electrical items near your car! Once again, I cannot stress enough, the need for **"Safety First"** in each and every transaction.

Chapter 10: **_Safety First (Continued)_**

Some people are out to take advantage of others. These unsavory characters can make this world of buying and selling look bad sometimes. Be careful not to carry a lot of cash with you or have valuable items with you when you're doing potential deals. Just protect yourself from strangers. I know this from personal experience, so I am just trying to protect you!

Chapter 11: **Investment Market, Side by Side Comparison.**

Investment	Risk	Interest Return	Time Frame
Checking Account	Low	<5%	Annual
Savings Account	Low	<5%	Annual
Money Mkt Account	Low	<5%	Annual
Certificate Of Deposit	Low	<5%	Annual
401K	Moderate	<15%	Annual
Savings Bond	Low	<12%	Annual
Real Estate	Moderate	<25%	Long Term
Gambling	High	(100% to (+) 10,000%	Day
Stocks	High	(100%) to 100%	Annual

Show me the Flippin Money!

	Low	50% to 500%	**Hourly, Daily, Weekly**

Chapter 12: *My Weekly Schedule (Example)*

Monday - The Hunt and Bread (Chapters 1 and 3)

I do this throughout the day at work, home, kids events, watching TV, and etc. I Make offers on all of my apps and Websites. I Make offers for 5-10 products on each app and websites I sometimes focus on all sites for the same items by using the search engines on these apps and websites or just look at all products information to negotiate price.

(Refer to Chapter 3 Constantly to get the upper hand in negotiations).

Tuesday – Bread and some Hunting (Chapters 3 and 1)

I do this throughout the day at work, home, kids events, watching TV, and etc. So easy to do but very important for my products to bee seen always. I also search to find more products to buy from my apps and websites.

Wednesday – Bread and some Hunting (Chapters 3 & 1)

I do this throughout the day at work, home, kids events, watching TV, and etc. So easy to do but very important for my products to bee seen always. I also search to find more products to buy from my apps and websites.

Thursday - The Hunt and Bread (Chapter 1 and 3)

I do this throughout the day at work, home, kids events, watching TV, and etc. I Make offers on all of my apps and Websites. I Make offers for 5-10 products on each app and websites I sometimes focus on all sites for the same items by using the search engines on these apps and websites or just look at all products information to negotiate price.

(Refer to Chapter 3 Constantly to get the upper hand in negotiations).

Friday – Bread and some Hunting (Chapters 1 and 3)

I do this throughout the day at work, home, kids events, watching TV, and etc. So easy to do but very important for my products to bee seen always. I also search to find more products to buy from my apps and websites.

Saturday--Bread & Hunting for local deals (Chapters 1 & 5)

This is a special day to do local close hunting deals. Yard, Garage, Moving, Estate, and chain store deals. This sometimes where you can find the best deals and people are willing to negotiate a lot to gain their space or to make quick money. Work these types of hunts the best you can to score out on some important inventory. Remember to post immediately for these items you buy because you will forget and even put it off. When you are doing this you can also bread your existing items.

Sunday - - You Decide Day

This is a day when you decide to do what is successful for you to do. I usually spent this day relaxing, doing the BREAD and playing with friends and getting ready for the upcoming week.

Chapter 13: **Whenever However Schedule.**

When I first started this business, I was thinking, "Well I don't want to be on other people's schedule" or "I really want to be able to do this business however *I* want to do it", so this is why I came up with the "Whenever However schedule".

This type of job is a "Whenever However schedule"- you can do this job from your car, at work, at home watching TV, or whenever you want to! Remember, this is a business that's part time income but it can help you make money on the side. There is no pre-set schedule. There is no boss. There is no punching in on a time clock. There are no tax deductions, angry customers, late nights, overnight shifts, early morning shifts, commutes, boring co-workers, or lay-offs. This is your life. Take control of it.

Chapter 13: **Whenever However Schedule (Continued)**

      Got a water bill that's due next week? Make some flips. Does your kid have a field trip that you must pay for? Make some flips. Short on rent? Make some flips! Wanna make some pocket money for the weekend? Someone just got their bi-weekly paycheck and they are looking for a deal on something.

    Make some flips! Whenever However! Make some easy money. Find a product to flip. Don't take a second job. You are the boss now!

Conclusion

I can tell you that I've made so many of these transactions- hunting and negotiating my profit, by sitting on the toilet, watching a movie, or eating. Even at work! This is a "Whatever, However-you-want-to-do-it kind of money maker. You have infinite amount of time that you can do this business; you can do this until you die!

I wanted to emphasize this. Flipping is a "whenever, however" business, so don't forget- when traveling around town and putting your own money and time into this business, the smart people don't travel far to buy and sell items. They don't engage in transactions that require them to travel far, you have to put in time, money *and* effort. Putting your time, money and effort into a transaction requires attention to detail. Every aspect of the deal can cut into your profits. Be very conservative, think smart! Your possible reward (profit) remains high as long as you follow the guidelines in this book. Have fun, stay motivated and make as much money as you can!

Conclusion (Continued)

I just want you know that I have had fun running this business for the last 15 years, and I have personally increased my cash flow for $300-$500 extra month during the slow time and $500-$3000 during the busy months. If you put my book to work you can have a constant cash flow of money and you will enjoy that constant cash flow.

I have treated this like a hobby, not as a second income job. It really is a second income job, but I have had fun with it and I love it! This, of course, is better than a part-time job, because if I had a part-time job in Corporate America, I would have to pay taxes and work crazy hours.

Flipping used items online is a simple business that I do part time, and I determine how much money I make. At the same time, I am helping others.

Conclusion (Continued)

I have so many personal stories that I can share with you. If you would like more information or even personal stories, you can email me and I will be glad to give you coaching, guidance, and inspiration! Happy Flipping!

Email: showmetheflippinmoney@gmail.com

My Collectible Flip.

(Case Study 1)

Day 1 Located items as WIIFB (4 baseball jerseys ($150) and $100 Cash for Autographed Helmet, Autographed Football, Autographed Basketball no COA's – Valued $1500 plus tax)

Day 1 Interested Party makes an offer to Trade 4 baseball jerseys ($150) and $100 Cash (Autographed, Helmet, Autographed Football, Autographed Basketball no COA' – Valued $1500)

Day 2 Met up at Location and made the deal. (Asked why trading. They love the Texas Rangers. Husband died and she was selling his items to make space in home other items.)

My Collectible Flip.

(Case Study 1-Continued)

Day 2	Create multiple posts – Posting $1500 (Websites and Apps)
Day 2-60	BREAD Process
Day 2-60	Reply/Negotiate
Day 2-60	BREAD Process
Day 2 – 60	WIIFS - Sold all three items for $1200. (475% return)

Case Study 1- Details

      First case study. This is the deal that started me in thinking that I can make money off of this website so I had some old Texas Ranger baseball jerseys that I no longer needed and I just wanted to get rid of. I had 4 Texas Rangers Jersey's and one autographed with no COA. Just regular baseball Texas Ranger jerseys with player names on them 3 of them and one with just an autograph of One of the Texas Ranger owners. I had a co-worker that went to a Texas Rangers game and he got me an autograph of the co-owner of the Texas Rangers. So, I posted the jerseys on a couple of websites and apps. A couple days after posting the ad somebody said they were interested. They were interested in a trade. I said what do you have? Well, this person came back and told me that she had an autographed helmet from the Cowboys and an autographed football form the Cowboys and also she had autographed basketball with a famous basketball player Shaquille O'Neil. I told her I'm interested in all three items.

Case Study 1 -Continued – Details

She came back and said it's not a fair trade but I'm a Rangers fan and how about the 4 jerseys and $100 Dollars. I did the math and it was only $150 bucks for the 4 jerseys for a total trade of maybe $250. Her total trade value was about $1500 worth of autographs. I quickly told her it's a deal. So we met up and she pulled up in a red Hummer. She looked at my stuff and I looked at her stuff and said OK let's do this. After the trade I asked her why are you trading this stuff. She said to me, well they were my husband's and he passed away a while ago. She was getting rid of his stuff because she had heritage a kaleidoscope collection that she wanted to put in place of of her husband's stuff.

This first trade was a big wow factor for me. I enjoyed showing it to all my family and friends. It was very exciting because at the same time I was able to make some awesome money. I sold all three items for around $1200. Making a 475% profit and paying no reported taxes.

Meet up in a safe place

My Smart Phone Flips.

(Case Study 2)

Day 1	Located items as WIIFB (Smartphone met up at AT&T store bought for $75 - Valued $175 plus tax)
Day 1	Buy Case and Charger ($20)
Day 1	Create multiple posts - Posted for $175 (Websites and Apps)
Day 2	BREAD Process
Day 2	Reply/Negotiate
Day 2	BREAD Process
Day 2	Interested Party makes an offer to buy Smartphone for $150
Day 2	Met up at Safe Location AT&T store and made the deal.
Day 2	WIIFS - Sold Smartphone $150 Profit $55. (150% return)

Case Study 2 – Details

I learned from prior case study transactions that I could shop for items and buy them cheap and then sell for a higher price. With this next item on Smartphones I found out when people were upgrading they needed to get rid of their old Smartphones so what they would do is advertise them on websites and resale apps. I would offer a very low price of $75 and it was accepted so after paying the $75 I then spent $10 to buy a case and $10 to buy a charger. I'm into it for $95. Smartphones for this type are selling on the market for around $175 so I started my price at $175 and then someone offered me $150. Well, I know that's not double my money but it's $55. What job can you find where you spend $95 and made $55 and not paying income taxes in less than 48 hours.

As I mentioned in Chapter 10 be careful when you buy Smartphones.

Case Study 2 -Continued – Details

Always meet up with the potential buyer at the telephone servicing company for safety and to check the IMEI codes. This is to check and see if it has been black marketed. Smartphones can be a big return if you just negotiate for a good price and add a couple cheap accessories. Stay strong on your price because you can make 150% or even 200% of your money back in less than 48 hours. I have been very successful doing Smartphone flips many times.

Meet up at a phone servicing company

My Garage Sale Item Flips.

(Case Study 3)

Day 1	Located items as WIIFB (Large Customized Dollhouse I bought for $75 and they delivered it for me- Valued $500)
Day 1	Create multiple posts – Posting for $400 (Websites and Apps)
Day 2	BREAD Process
Day 2-5	Reply/Negotiate
Day 2-5	BREAD Process
Day 6	Interested Party makes an offer of trade for $200 cash and 10 antique plates.
Day 6	Met up at Safe location and made the trade.
Day 6	WIIFS – Traded for $200 cash and 10 antique plates (275% return and kept antique plates)

Case Study 3 - *Details*

    This case study I bought a very large dollhouse that was electrically wired in every small detailed room. This miniature dollhouse was almost as big as a small kitchen island. It was very dusty and it needed a little TLC. I knew this when I bought it from the garage for $75. I got a great deal for $75 because the prior owner helped deliver it to my home. WOW even a better deal!! I painted the dollhouse and I fixed it up a little with some TLC. As I was fixing it up I was marketing the item on my websites and resale apps. Within two months of owning it I sold it
and made a couple hundred dollars of cash and 10 antique plates. As of today I still have these plates and I plan to keep them because they are beautiful. Oh and I was really thinking about keeping the dollhouse for fun. I made more than my $75 back and also have 10 antique plates.

Case Study 3 – Continued - *Details*

I attend lots of garage sales, yard sales, moving sales, estate sales, and etc. I have been very successful as a WIIFB/WIIFS on selling my items on websites and my apps. I do this on a constant basis and I spend little money buying things but I make a lot of money in flipping. I would recommend starting your flipping business with buying items at these events. Its one of the easiest ways to double or triple your money. You can find many items at one stop. For example, you spend $20 dollars but you can make $60 to $80. To be successful in
making the most of your items try to buy items that are in new condition, need little TLC, and don't take up too much space.

Meet up in a safe place

My Smart Pad Flips.

(Case study 4)

Day 1	Located items as WIIFB - (Bought Smart Pad for $50- Valued $150)
Day 1	Create multiple posts – Posting for $150 (Websites and Apps)
Day 2	BREAD Process
Day 2	Interested Party makes an offer $140
Day 3	Met up at Safe Location and made the deal.
Day 3	WIIFS - Sold for $140. Profit $90 (285% return)

Case study 4 - Details

In this case study I learned from my Smartphone deal. Since I could do this in the prior deal I thought Smart Pads are really popular with adults, teenagers, kids, and business's. So I decided to research on how much I could get a Smart Pad for. Well these things were selling between $150 - $200 for the ones that were in good condition with a charger and a case. In reviewing the Smart Pad field, I realized the market was flooded with them. So many Smart Pads on the market so I just started to make crazy offers on a lot of them. I bought a good one for $50 I then sold it in 3 days for $140 not bad for a $50 investment that's $90 profit for a 275% profit.

    I loved the first deal so much that I purchased another one for $50 and kept if for myself. After buying one for myself I then have completed many Smart Pad flips.

Case study 4 – Continued - Details

This is one of the easiest transactions to make quick money plus you can use the Smart Pad temporarily until you sell it. You should always meet up in a place that has Wi-Fi and activate the product with your account information. You don't want to by a stolen or a bad product. Test drive the item.

*** Meet up in a safe pace and activate it with your account**

My Road/Mtn Bike Deal/Flips.

(Case Study 5)

Day 1   Located items as WIIFB/WIIFS (Bought Road Bike for $450 - Valued $700)

(Case Study 5) Details

In this case study you will learn why I bought a road bike. About 9 years ago my weight was around 225 pounds I felt very tired and I did not look that good. So I heard that lots of people started biking to lose the weight. I thought of helping myself with exercising on a road bike. I decided to buy a road bike so I took some of my cash that I've made from the transactions and negotiated a 700 Dollar bike specialized. I negotiated to $450. I explained to the seller that I had to lose weight because of my fatigue and I did not look healthy. After buying the road bike I lost a lot of weight and now am healthy and I look great!! I could sell the road bike for around $600 but I love it.

Case Study 5 - Details

I have bought and sold a couple MTN and Road bikes for real low prices and sold them for higher prices. Remember to be careful in buying bikes. Make sure they're in good quality with no problems like no rust and they don't need much TLC. If you can do this correctly, you can flip these and make a good profit. This flip is a seasonal item and you should buy a couple of months before the season comes and then you sell high when it is in season. You don't want to buy too many because then you have to store them in a good place to protect them from the elements.

Meet up in a safe place

My Television Flips.

(Case Study 6)

Day 1	Located items as WIIFB (Bought TV for $50 - Valued $150-$200)
Day 1	Create multiple posts – Posting for $150 (Websites and Apps)
Day 2	BREAD Process
Day 2	Reply/Negotiate
Day 3	BREAD Process
Day 3	Interested Party makes an offer to buy TV for $135.
Day 3	Met up at Safe Location and made the deal.
Day 4	WIIFS - Sold for $135 – Profit $85. (1000% return)

Case Study 6 – Details

I personally did this at first because I had an old 32 inch Visio TV LCD and I wanted to get a bigger TV for my master bedroom so I decided to go out and try to see if I can find a bigger TV. I ended up selling my older 32" TV for $75 and I bought a 55" TV for $75 but the prior owner was selling it for $150. After being successful personally I found another 32" TV just a couple miles away from my house. A gentleman was selling it for $100 wow! I put my skills to work and I offered him $50 so he accepted and I went and picked it up so I then put the 32" TV on the market for $150. I put my plan to work and I ended up selling it for $135. So really for my $50 investment I made $85 profit. After doing the last 2 TV deals I decided to sell my old Samsung DLP 50" projection TV. I ended up selling selling it for $100. It was a piece of outdated junk but somebody bought it but with my talented marketing skills.

Case Study 6 – Continued - Details

I have had much success in doing these TV flips with a friend of mine and aby myself. I have made a lot of money doing this flip. The reason this flip is so easy to do is because people are always wanting to upgrade and they need to get rid of the old models. The old models still have value to another person who need them for man cave, child's room, or another room in the home. TV's are very important for people so they can watch all of their shows, sporting events, play, and for looks. The electronics movement on TV comes in waves and you can flip them prior to a big event. Just learn to plan ahead and you will be able to make big profits on this. The TV market is as big as the car market is. So don't just sit back and watch get Flippin.

When buying a TV remember to test it and if no remote with it negotiate for a way lower price and go buy a $10 remote. This will will help in selling the TV for a higher value.

Case Study 6 – Continued - Details

Do not buy TV's that have damage or don't turn on or if the seller gives you an excuse. Don't get burned on this and if you do then you still can get some of your money back by selling it for parts but It is difficult to do that an you will have to sit on it until a unique person buys it for that reason. Do not buy to many TV's at once then you have to store them. I only do a couple at a time.

Meet up in a safe place to test TV and to sell TV.

My Free Item Flips.

(Case Study 7)

Day 1	Located items as WIIFB (Bought for **Free** - Valued $1-$200)
Day 1	Create multiple posts – Posted for $1-$200 (Websites and Apps)
Day 1	BREAD Process
Day 2	Reply/Negotiate
Day 2	BREAD Process
Day 2	Interested Party makes an offer to me for $1-$200
Day 3	Met up at Safe Location and make the deal.
Day 3	WIIFS - Sold all for $1-$200. (Giant return)

Case Study 7 - Details

In this case study you will learn to look for free items on apps and websites. These apps and websites have lots of free items and they have their own category for Free Items. Locate this category on the apps and websites. So much to be made from others giving it away for free. One person's trash is another person's treasure. Some of these items will be in good condition but remember some of these free items just need a little TLC. Using the skills taught in my book you will turn these items into 100%, 200%, 300%, and etc. profits.

Here is an example for a free item. I drove 2 cities over and picked up a 12 foot Christmas tree and I got it for free. I had to drive about 5 miles to pick it up I picked it up I put my skills to work and I ended up selling the Christmas tree for $150 and I did all this within 48 hours this is just what you can do with all of the free. Remember one person's trash is another person's treasure.

<u>Case Study 7 – Continued - Details</u>

This is probably the simplest ways to make quick money. So if you are desperately needing some money I would recommend doing these kinds of flips and if you put the skills taught to you in this book it will be easy money and you don't have to risk any of your money because the items are free.

Meet up in a safe place

Big Crazy Item Flips.

(Case Study 8)

Day 1	Located items as WIIFB (Bought Pool Table/Ping Pong Table for $75 - Valued $400)
Day 1	Create multiple posts – Posting for $350 (Websites and Apps)
Day 2	BREAD Process
Day 2	Reply/Negotiate
Day 3	BREAD Process
Day 3	Interested Party makes an offer to me for $300.
Day 4	Met up at Safe Location and made the deal.
Day 5	WIIFS - Sold items for $300. (400% return)

Case Study 8 - Details

In this case study you will learn of a big item flip. People are always getting rid of big items all of the time do to changing events in their lives. You will be amazed at this one I did. I was searching on my websites and apps and I found a pool table/ping pong table that somebody just wanted to get rid of and they were only selling it for $75. So I said to them I can come and pick it up right now. I drove2 0 minutes and I borrowed a truck from my friend and I picked it up. I was planning on keeping it so I then played around with it for a couple days. My wife said to me we really don't have the space for this and it's an item we really don't need. So I ended up putting it out on my sites and apps for $350 with in 48 hours someone offered me $300.

I accepted the offer and therefore my $75 turned into $300 that's a $225 profit. Turning 75 into $300.

Case Study 8 – Continued - Details

That gives you a 400% return in actuality only a 300% return because you had to put $75 of your own money into it but that is an awesome return and there are deals out there that people are willing to do for you because you are helping them get rid of an item they no longer need and one less thing they have to worry about.

Meet up in a safe place

Glossary of Acronyms.

WIIFB

"What's In It For Buyer?"

WIIFS

"What's In It For Seller?"

WIIFM

"What's In It For Me"

BREAD

"**B**oost, **R**eboot, **E**dit, **A**dd, and **D**elete."

"The Excitement of Flippin Wow!"

--M.B. KIM

Thank you for buying my book.

www.ingramcontent.com/pod-product-compliance
Lightning Source LLC
Chambersburg PA
CBHW030946240526
45463CB00016B/1980